MOUNTAIN LIFE

A Rocky Mountain Guide to Elevated Living

JEFF PASQUALE

ISBN: 978-0-9896603-5-8

Edited by Mary Hoekstra (writeandeditright5@gmail.com)
Text layout and design by Fagaras Codrut Sebastian (fagaras.office@gmail.com)
Life series cover concept by Maura Pasquale
Cover design by Stacey Lane Design (http://www.staceylanedesign.com/)

Designed in and inspired by Colorado

For my wife, Maura Pasquale,
who willingly traveled across the country
with me for this Colorado journey.

CONTENTS

INTRODUCTION

The world desperately needs inspiration.

Admit it. When was the last time you felt inspired? Not the inspiration you get from a movie or news sound bites, but a real "this makes me want to be a better person" kind of kick in the pants.

Inspiration comes in many forms—people, places, and things. My inspiration comes from the mountains.

After living in South Florida for nearly thirty years, I left its subtropical environment for the semiarid climate of Denver, Colorado. Less than twenty-four hours after arriving there, I headed to my first day on my new job. After a few miles of driving, I reached a high point, and the road opened before my eyes . . . and so did the view of the Rocky Mountains and their Front Range, from Pikes Peak to Longs Peak.

On this comfortably cool June morning, the sun was striking the mountains broadside. The distinctively brown lower foothills were the perfect contrast to the white-peaked mountains rising behind them. The sight of Mount Evans, the tallest, most distinctive peak in view, was stunning.

My arrival in Colorado marked several milestones besides a new state residence; it marked a new position in a new industry and a new sense of adventure. The biggest discovery, once I settled in, was the people. The spirit of the people of the Front Range and the Denver metropolitan area is as unique as the view of the Rockies. People who live on the Front Range possess a refreshing blend of optimism, persistence, inclusiveness, and determination, and a fiercely independent and interdependent spirit.

That first morning drive spotlighted the power and depth of the Rockies and became my constant reminder we're not going to be here forever, so we should appreciate the view.

We all process things differently. One person could be standing on a fourteen-thousand-foot mountaintop in awe of the view, and another might be checking his cell phone for a signal. Most people, however, will stand that high in the sky and be awestruck; only a minority will be unmoved or preoccupied with something totally unrelated to their surroundings. Almost universally, the Rocky Mountains generate powerful feelings of amazement and wonder.

Mountains inspire. They have been an obvious source of inspiration since mankind first gazed upon them. They produce lofty feelings that never go away. Each time you ascend a mountaintop and gaze from its heights upon the vastness around you, your senses are overcome by the sights and sounds (almost none), and even the crispness of the air.

Atop a mountain, it's easy to forget your problems and concerns. The limitlessness and scope of its vistas are captivating and can soon obliterate any worries or concerns you may have had on the climb up. As you survey the terrain below, you may realize your problems will never be as big as this . . . not as big as this mountain, not as big as this moment, and not as big as this panorama around you.

Being on a mountaintop is an instant mood-changer. A forty-five-minute drive to the mountains from the city, for example, will provide even the most ardent city dweller an opportunity to stand amidst real canyons versus concrete ones.

Most people don't live in or near mountains, though; they reside at sea level and consequently must deal with the challenges city living frequently generates in their lives. Whether you live in the city or the mountains, it's very likely you wish for a little more structure, balance, and peace in your life.

Many of us have a compulsion for distraction, which makes our lives a little more difficult and complex because we're not paying attention to what's happening in front of us.

We've all heard life can be as simple or as complex as we make it. With that in mind, one of the principal intentions of *Mountain Life* is to help you close the gap between the simple and complex elements in your life. As you read, my intention is to show you how to access your sources of strength, inspiration, and peace, and to help you realize and experience more meaning in your life.

Mountain Life is about the land and the people of Colorado, the Rocky Mountains, and the Front Range.

Living in the mountains occasionally involves a small degree of risk, so *Mountain Life* also contains stories about everyday problems we all face.

The environment we live in surrounds our public and private experiences, and it also specifies how we interact with it (as in the mountains). When you live in the mountains, you don't have much choice but to contend with the ever-changing, ever-challenging terrain and climate. The overarching environment of the mountains always prevails over everything else.

Mountain life is not oppressive. In fact, it's usually quite the opposite. Life in the mountains is full of opportunities ... to explore, to share, to indulge, to learn, and to have fun. At the end of the day, no matter where we live, it's how we respond to people, situations, and our surroundings that define who we are as individuals and as members of our community. **Our responses define our lives.**

Mountain life offers an abundance of the *alone time* if we seek it. It may be hard for some to envision spending time without other people, but sometimes that's exactly what we need to do . . . not for days or weeks but sometimes for just a few hours.

Many of us need to relearn how to be alone with ourselves and our thoughts. That desire to be alone is why solo hikers tread through sagebrush and scree, why climbers hang by their fingertips in the blazing sun, and why runners trek through tall grass and paths with towering evergreens. There is a different kind of bonding taking place at such times ... just not with people.

The mountains are sacred. The North American Indians refer to places like the Rockies as sacred ground, which means the land and environment are considered as important as a living being and are deserving of the same respect, honor, and consideration.

People choose the mountains as their home precisely because it's an opportunity to see how life is interconnected. The fun and adventure, the occasional dangers, the ups, the downs, the heat and cold are all here to experience and enjoy.

Living in the mountains affords us the ability to enhance and support a healthier lifestyle, but we don't need to physically live near mountains to experience mountain life. Even a short visit will offer experiences that inspire us and bring out our best. Those experiences will stay with us long after we've returned home.

The secret to mountain life (and life in general) is developing deeper connections with as many things as you can. This includes you yourself, other people, and the land and space you inhabit. It sounds easy, but it takes practice to learn how to make those connections in a meaningful way.

Mountain life is a life with less stress, fewer hassles, and more appreciation for the good things around you. I know this sounds a bit unrealistic. It's not.

So if you're a skeptical, cynical, or too-busy type of person, it may be worth an elevated experience in the mountains to change your perspective on things.

I | ATTITUDE

Attitude is a state of mind. A positive attitude is highly contagious and changes lives for the better.

Determination is not measured by the goals we achieve
but by the actions we take in pursuit of those goals.

What a great trait to possess!

With determination, discoveries are made, scientific breakthroughs are accomplished, and seemingly impossible tasks are completed.

Determination is a combination of purpose, resolve, and focus. Yes, there are other ingredients, but these three seem to dominate the behaviors of history's most accomplished achievers.

The mountains portray determination by their presence, persevering from millennium after millennium. But this is where the comparison ends. Mostly, mountains represent the determination of people who choose to hike, bike, climb, and ski them.

Hiking up a steep mountain trail, for example, requires determination, with equal amounts of purpose, resolve, and focus.

The intrepid hiker could be going it alone or in a group, but sooner or later the expedition becomes a contest solely between the hiker and the mountain. That contest begins quickly if the climber is ascending one of Colorado's fifty-six mountains rising higher than fourteen thousand feet. (*Fourteeners*, as they're called.)

In everyday life, determination is needed for a variety of reasons. Whether you're creating a new company or growing an existing one, fighting the flu or combating a debilitating disease, a certain amount of determination is always required. The seeds of determination exist within each of us. Our mission is to locate those seeds, nurture them, and allow them to germinate.

Determination is a necessary trait we all need to move our lives forward. Unless we have engaged in a great deal of self-reflection and self-convincing, most of us don't go out of our way to engage in activities requiring extreme effort without relying upon determination.

Determination is measured not just by the goals we achieve but also by the actions we take in pursuit of those goals. Use determination to your benefit. When you are more conscious of just how determined you are, you may actually increase that determination.

Replay

- Hiking up a steep mountain trail requires determination, with equal amounts of purpose, resolve, and focus.
- Determination is a necessary trait we all need to move our lives forward.

Action to Take / Questions to Ponder

What does determination look like in your life? Think of a situation in which you were cornered and had to shift into determination immediately. What are you now determined to do? Where are you determined to work, live, or visit?

*Gratitude gets us out of our heads and
back into our hearts.*

A mountain is just a rock; it has no capacity for gratitude. Some people are just as limited, but we all have the ability to appreciate things, such as being grateful for the grandeur and beauty of a mountain.

So here's the thing: if gratitude is so easy, why is it so hard for us to consistently be thankful for the things we have in our lives? We struggle to appreciate or be grateful for things like relationships, jobs, accomplishments, possessions, or simply being alive.

A friend confided he was feeling a little depressed because it was his birthday. He said it made him feel like his life was swiftly passing him by. It was a simple admission, but it struck me because I could not relate to it. Maybe I'm very blessed (which I know I am), but even on my worst days, I manage to find something to be grateful for.

It's become an automatic response for many of us to fixate on our problems. Today's society presumes there is something wrong with us if we're not worrying or obsessing about what we don't have, what might happen, or what we might miss out on.

It's time to start feeling more and thinking less. Gratitude gets us out of our heads and back into our hearts.

Some personal coaches use an exercise that begins with the question, "What are you most proud of?" Usual responses from clients include their children, marrying their spouse, or their accomplishments at work. We should ask ourselves the same question when we catch ourselves complaining or feeling bad. It will help us move away from feeling sorry for ourselves towards gratefulness.

Gratitude is a learned response, but it requires conscious effort. With practice, this learned response becomes the trigger for conscious, constant gratitude.

In extreme situations, when we feel our world might be falling apart, being grateful is the last thing we think about ... unless we've learned how to do it automatically.

When gratitude is an automatic response, we begin to feel our lives are less troubled, less precarious.

We must train ourselves in the art of conscious gratitude. It gets us back on track when we most need to and shift our focus from negative to positive in a matter of seconds. When gratitude exists, even the small things in life can have a big positive impact on us.

Replay

- Gratitude is a learned response.
- It's time to start feeling more and thinking less.

Action to Take / Questions to Ponder

Try embracing and practicing gratitude for one day. Think about how you will accomplish that challenge. At the end of the day, reflect on how your gratitude affected you and all you did.

Peaks afford us a unique view and perspective by temporarily
releasing us from the stress of accomplishing, pushing,
or climbing.

W hen we are at a peak, regardless of what kind, our
perspective changes.

Obviously, peaks can be reached in life without
climbing a mountain. A peak could be attaining a higher
level of popularity, performance, or accomplishment,
or reaching an increased level of health, insight,
or knowledge.

When we view things from the elevated perspective
of a peak, our senses, thoughts, and emotions are
heightened as well. From such a height, what we see can
be breathtaking and surreal because it's a vista we don't
normally behold.

We all experience peaks in life. While they may vary
in degrees from person to person, the feeling is the same.

When we are at a peak, it's easy to feel as if we are on top of the world. As time passes, we may start to believe our situation is normal and things will remain this way. This is a trap we all can fall into: becoming complacent, aloof, or indifferent.

One way to avoid this trap is to practice gratitude.

Like a climber atop a tall mountain who stops to appreciate the view, we must all savor the moment or the accomplishment regardless of the peak we have scaled.

Peaks afford us a unique view and perspective by temporarily releasing us from the stress of accomplishing, pushing, or climbing. This unique perspective from the top offers us the opportunity to learn and appreciate. It's a privilege to be up there. Appreciate the view. Avoid taking it for granted.

Replay

- When we are at a peak, our perspective changes.
- When we are at a peak, it's easy to believe things will always be like this, but they won't!

Action to Take / Questions to Ponder

When did you last feel you were at a peak? How did that influence the decisions you made at the time?

Stubbornness is a choice.

Without question, mountains are immovable. Even when explosives are employed, a mountain may crumble a bit, but it's not going anywhere. A mountain is steadfast, as predictable as the sun in the sky. With people, it's different.

We all know at least one person who prides himself on his immovability; stubbornness is his badge of honor.

Stubborn folks enjoy comparing themselves to the unyielding image of a mountain, and they like projecting that same image. They subscribe to the tenet that nothing can move them from their position. They refuse to change their minds, their beliefs, or their attitudes because they find comfort in their buffer of immovability.

People who are so unyielding seem gladdened by the attention. They want the recognition. They feel validated.

Years ago, we called them cranky people; now we know better. Cranky people clearly like the attention they garner from their stubbornness. It's safe to assume that people who consistently go out of their way to be unyielding have bigger problems than whatever they're being stubborn about. Here's the thing, though: stubborn people are rarely happy or upbeat individuals. In fact, they're just the opposite.

Most of us enjoy a good challenge now and again. We'll banter; we'll joust; we may even get a little loud in the process. Most times, it's just harmless posturing. Our competitive spirit gets the better of us, we engage, and then we forget about it. There are times, though, when we must take a stand for something we feel strongly about. That is not being stubborn; it's being smart. But it takes time and wisdom to learn the subtle differences between the two.

The trait of immovability can be viewed two ways: it can be highly admirable, or it can be a huge liability.

Stubbornness is a choice. We can choose to be immovable like a mountain when situations require, or we can live a life of ongoing stress and conflict by resisting every issue we face—big or small. The latter sounds like a lot of work.

Replay

- Immovability can be viewed as admirable or as a liability.
- Years ago, we called them cranky people; now we know better.

Action to Take / Questions to Ponder

How can you tell when you're being stubborn versus standing up for something you value? What prompts you to become stubborn? What calls you to stand up?

We choose wandering in order to learn, to discover,
or to escape from the predictability of our lives.

Exploring could easily be counted as an official activity of Colorado, right along with skiing, biking, and hiking, to name just a few. Everywhere you look, especially in and around the Front Range, people are wandering around, exploring new spaces, or engaging in activities requiring them to get on their feet, on a bike, on a horse, or on a skateboard, or to strap on their skis.

The great part about wandering the mountains of Colorado is there are so many of them, and all possess a multitude of trails, roads, and slopes to conquer.

Wandering has played a significant role in our lives. Without the urge to wander, no one would have left the Old World to discover the New World, ventured to locate the North Pole, or sought a new route to the East. Wandering is practically a genetic predisposition for many of us; those with that gene can't sit still, whether we are eight or eighty.

Wandering stretches our muscles and minds, requires us to think, plan, and do . . . and eventually to come back home. We choose wandering in order to learn, to discover, or to escape from the predictability of our lives. The reason for our wandering is not as important as the fact we *are* wandering.

Wandering doesn't mean we must leave home. Wandering isn't only about physical movement. We use our minds to wander through books and other media sources to explore and discover.

Blaise Pascal (1623–1662), French mathematician and philosopher said, "Our nature is in movement: complete calm is death."

A sobering thought, but if we are honest with ourselves, it makes sense. A full life is one of motion.

So come to the mountains. Wander more. Explore more. See more. Feel more. And then return home with a new constructive, positive habit. Wander!

Replay

- The reason for our wandering is not as important as the fact we *are* wandering.
- A full life is one of motion.

Action to Take / Questions to Ponder

Play with the concept of wandering as much as you can. Wander in your car, on your bike, on your feet, or in your mind and imagination.

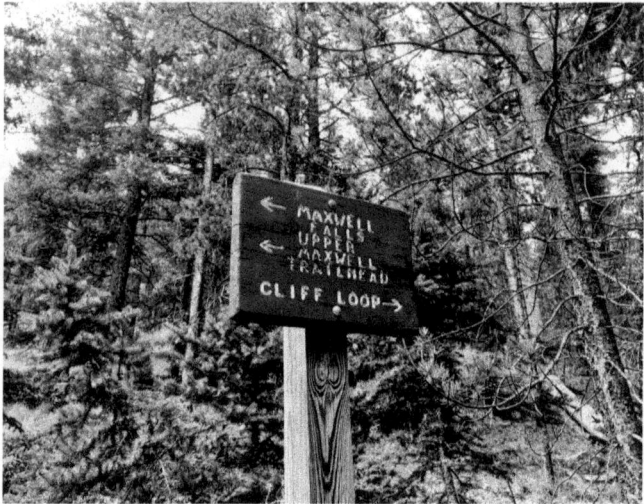

II | DISCERNMENT

Are you aware or adrift?

How well do you see, perceive, and
understand people and things around you?

Whether we live in the mountains or in midtown, it's important to dig deeper, ask more questions, and challenge the status quo.

Things are not always what they appear to be, so we must develop a talent for discerning the truth from something that masquerades as the truth.

Every day, we accept most things at face value and move on. About 90 percent of what we perceive is routine, mundane, or of no consequence; most things do not require our full attention. For that remaining 10 percent, it's important to stop and seek clarification. Why? Because our tendency is to make assumptions as we go through life. These daily assumptions make life easier; that's how most of us get through our day.

Those assumptions address the routine things in life: we assume our food is safe, our drink is clean, and the plane we fly in has had proper maintenance.

Whether we live in the mountains or in midtown, it's important to dig deeper, ask more questions, and challenge the status quo. That does not mean we're rebellious. In fact, it's quite the opposite. It means we're prudent.

Marketers depend on us to believe their stories. They stretch the truth just enough to make their products sound irresistible, amazing, and worth buying. We really do want to believe some things are true and good.

Think about the diet pill that claims quick, permanent weight loss; the cream that magically removes wrinkles; or the vitamin that increases stamina. If only we'd asked a few more questions or worked harder to uncover the truth, we probably would have found that things were not as they seemed when they first appeared before our eager eyes.

A good example is a delicacy named Rocky Mountain oysters. They're on the menu of many a restaurant throughout Colorado. People regularly consume them . . . but they're not oysters. Not even close. They have a cool name and a bit of a mystique, so the fable about them continues. No one is harmed, but if you eat them and later find out what they really are, you may take pause before consuming them again.

Why are they called Rocky Mountain oysters? Because if you were told what they really were, you probably wouldn't eat them.

Whether it's everyday life or we're hiking in the mountains, clarifying instead of assuming helps us choose which path is better to travel or whether we really do want to try those "oysters."

Replay

- Ninety percent of what we perceive is routine or mundane. For that remaining 10 percent, it's important to stop and seek clarification.
- Our daily assumptions make life easier, but we still need to ask questions.

Action to Take / Questions to Ponder

Describe a time when you made an incorrect assumption about something (or someone) and it surprised you. Describe a time you were discerning and it prevented a lot of problems for you.

Scarcity has two distinct meanings, and both make
living difficult.

Scarcity is a reality for people living in or near
the mountains. The basics of life—food, water,
and shelter—are sometimes at risk on a mountain.
Hailstorms, flash floods, and blizzards all have the
potential to create short-term scarcity, even where food,
water, and shelter may abound at other times.

When a road gets snowed under or washed out from
a flash flood, the typical response is to take a different
route. In the mountains, it's different. There are not a
lot of alternate roads or sidewalks; options are scarce.
Living in the mountains is not necessarily dangerous,
but it certainly contrasts with living in lower elevations.

A surprise blizzard in any northern climate is capable
of separating people from work, from the grocery store,
or from one another, but that isn't the same as living

in the mountains. Living here will give you pause to appreciate what you have and to recognize how easy it is to suddenly be without.

Scarcity has two distinct meanings, and both make living difficult. First, scarcity defines a need for a commodity (food, water, money, etc.) in short supply. Second, scarcity represents the mindset or belief there will never be enough regardless if quantities are plentiful; it's the perception of scarcity that affects people.

Scarcity forces us to recognize how badly we need or want something, which usually creates the motivation to take immediate action.

We experience another form of scarcity when we first visit the mountains: less oxygen. In that case, scarcity helps us appreciate something a lot of us take for granted—being able to breathe without difficulty.

The good thing about scarcity is it eventually leads us to a point of gratefulness for what we do have even when there's not enough. Scarcity helps us be more discerning in life. As a result, we make better choices, and we find it easier to appreciate what we have.

Replay

- Scarcity forces us to recognize how badly we need or want something.
- The good thing about scarcity is it eventually leads us to a point of gratefulness.

Action to Take / Questions to Ponder

How does scarcity help you be more discerning and mindful in your everyday life?

Actions like keeping our word and always doing our best
tend to have the biggest influence on the level of our certainty.

We have all experienced certainty in our lives, whether it was about a decision we made or a belief we had. There was no doubt about how we felt. We were certain, and we had an overpowering belief we were right.

A mountain also conveys a strong degree of certainty by its presence. It remains a presence, day in and day out. We have no doubt the mountain will be there tomorrow.

Regarding people, though, a significant percentage of us are walking contradictions. One day we're crying foul that someone has cheated the system or broken a rule, and the next day we're committing the very same transgression. Somehow we've managed to justify our actions with certainty.

Now here's the funny part: we have little trouble spotting everyone else's missteps, yet we have difficulty recognizing our own. What's funnier is our certainty we are correct. Having a sense of certainty is comforting, especially if we sense something good is going to happen. Most of us want more certainty in our lives.

Certainty is an elusive goal we want but sometimes struggle to attain. It can be a fleeting experience for some of us. There will be times when we are fearless, believing nothing can stop us, but then, moments later, circumstances or moods change and we're as vulnerable as an ant crossing a busy intersection.

We all know almost nothing is certain. Yet we are still surprised when we struggle to control events in our lives.

We do have control, however, over how we feel. Actions, like keeping our word and always doing our best, tend to have the biggest influence on our feeling of certainty. By living this way, we become more like a mountain—steadfast and predictable.

Replay

- Certainty is the overpowering belief we are correct.

- We have difficulty recognizing our own missteps, yet we have little trouble spotting everyone else's.

Action to Take / Questions to Ponder

Do you reach a point of certainty about things too easily or too quickly?

Do you jump to the conclusions you want and latch onto them, hoping they happen? Do you need to consider modifying this tendency?

It's the small things we do that have the biggest impacts on our lives and on the lives of others.

The mountains evoke a certain amount of wonder and awe in all of us. Their immensity and presence inspire us to think big and act big, as if we too were larger than life and invincible. This is a good thing, but there are also times when we should recognize our limitations. It is not necessary to live in a larger-than-life fashion in order to accomplish great things.

Many times it's the small things we do that have the biggest impacts on our lives and on the lives of others. The helping hand, the knowing smile, or the gracious gesture take little effort, yet they can yield great dividends.

Allow yourself to feel small and insignificant occasionally. It's a simple way to get grounded and centered. When you look up at the stars, it's easy to imagine yourself as a speck of dust in the universe. The intent is to momentarily distance yourself from your earthly connections. It's also a way to stop you from feeling so damned important.

The point is, in the universe of things, we're really not that big. We seldom think about the size of the stars and solar systems that surround us. For example, the sun is so big, it could fit 1,300,000 Earths inside of it. Being conscious of just how small the earth (and each of us) is compared to the sun is another way of becoming aware of the reality of smallness in our lives.

Recognizing our insignificance may even humble us for a moment. While there is nothing wrong with feeling important (we all have egos), when we start believing we're better than others, things begin to go astray. Our self-importance (or imagined bigness) makes us feel that we're much larger than we really are.

Smallness reconnects us to the world in ways we usually don't perceive because we're too busy being busy. Don't misunderstand. It's a good thing to think big and be action-oriented, but it's just as crucial to learn how to step back and consider the bigger picture . . . the world and our small but impactful role in it. Humility has its place.

Replay

- It is not necessary to live in a larger-than-life fashion in order to accomplish great things.
- In the universe of things, we're really not that big.

Action to Take / Questions to Ponder

How do you keep yourself grounded?

III | CIRCUMSTANCES

"It is what it is," as the saying goes, but circumstances are much more than that. Circumstances give us perspective and help us to respond more effectively.

Obscurity in life can leave us feeling lost, alone, or detached from the outside world.

Obscurity in the mountains occurs because of external factors; clouds, snow, or smog fade or cover the view. Life has its own version of obscurity.

Obscurity is a situation we usually try to avoid. It affects our vision and our ability to perceive things. Obscurity can exist whether we're looking at the mountains or evaluating a life challenge.

Obscurity in life occurs when conditions have made it hard for us to see things clearly. Things like stress, deadlines, or emotional pain will disorient us.

When obscurity occurs in our personal lives, our first impulse might be to spend time determining its cause instead of addressing the fact we're not perceiving things clearly.

Obscurity in life can leave us feeling lost, alone, or detached from the outside world. It can make us feel *disconnected* from the people or things we care deeply about. The result is we struggle to relate effectively to others.

We must learn to recognize when the haze of obscurity is developing in our lives.

Identifying the onset of obscurity doesn't guarantee we'll find a solution, but like slowing when driving into fog, it may buy us some time to consider our options before we're in the thick of things.

When obscurity finds us, the best we can do is recognize we're not seeing things clearly and then consciously make the best choices we can.

Replay

- Identifying the onset of obscurity doesn't guarantee we'll find a solution, but it may allow us to buy some time to consider our options before we're in the thick of things.
- Obscurity in life can leave us feeling lost, alone, or detached from the outside world.

Action to Take / Questions to Ponder

Where does obscurity typically appear in your life?

Silence is a gift; we should take advantage
of it regularly.

Silence is a dominant presence in the mountains. People living on the Front Range prefer to seek solace in the mountains because of the silence they afford.

There are fewer distracting sounds up there . . . no music, no rattling railroad cars, no blasting car horns, and no screaming police sirens. Just peace.

Except for the occasional snap of a branch, rustle of leaves, or screech of a bird, soundlessness pervades in the mountains. For people, however, soundlessness seems harder to come by.

Not everyone seeks silence. There are also people who prefer the noise and distraction of civilization.

The individuals who avoid silence appear more at ease with noises generated electronically than with the solitude of a book, a newspaper, or meditation. For some, the need to be preoccupied is strong.

Silence can be a spiritual experience, be it in the mountains, the desert, or the plains. There is something powerfully profound in the simple act of being alone.

Deliberate silence is also a powerful medicament if you are struggling to gain clarity in your life. The sound of silence enhances our ability to recognize the simplicity of things. In other words, silence is an opportunity for us to unplug.

This is one of life's biggest challenges: being able to silence the mind as well as the environment.

Silence is a gift. We should take advantage of it regularly. We don't have to travel to the mountains to experience it . . . but it doesn't hurt.

Replay

- Forced silence is a powerful medicament when we are struggling to gain clarity in our lives.
- Silence is a dominant presence in the mountains.

Action to Take / Questions to Ponder

In what ways could you introduce silence more regularly in your life?

Action Backfires! (Questions to Ponder)

8. Who were some you met today? Is it more reality of your life?

One absolute to being snowed under—at some point
we must start digging.

It's probably not surprising to hear that most people living in the mountains don't mind getting snowed under. They wouldn't be living there if they did.

For those who don't live in the mountains (or the northern latitudes), *snowed under* has very different meanings, oftentimes with serious connotations. To them, it could mean being buried in something—work, problems, or debt—so the term doesn't always evoke good feelings.

Meanwhile, back in the mountains, being snowed under has even more meanings, and nearly all of them relate to having fun. Skiing, snowboarding, snowmobiling, snowman-building, and sledding are activities that being snowed under promises mountain dwellers.

In the mountains, we can and should enjoy being snowed under in winter. It is essential to finding ways to have fun, relax, and take in the white solitude.

One absolute to being snowed under: at some point we must start digging. This is not to be flippant; it's the truth. Each of us has to dig ourselves out of the piles (of work, problems, or challenges) that occasionally surround us. There is no other realistic option, except maybe running away.

Sooner or later, though, you're going to have to shovel your sidewalk, get through the pile of work on your desk, or return all the calls you've been avoiding.

Sometimes the best course of action is to take a breather and determine what you're going to do once the storm has passed and you're ready to do some work.

Replay

- Sooner or later, though, you're going to have to shovel your sidewalk.
- To be snowed under can be serious, like being buried in work, problems, or debt.

Action to Take / Questions to Ponder

Describe your best response to being snowed under with work or other life situations.

The ledge is all about the view; it may be one you'll always cherish or one you wish you could forget.

We've all been on ledges before. The ledge is the place where the risk is high, the reward may be questionable, and the position can be precarious. If we lean one way, we might fall off; if we step back, we'll be out of danger, but the view won't be the same.

If you haven't figured it out already, the ledge is all about the view.

Keep in mind that the view might be one you'll always cherish or one you'll wish you could forget. A ledge offers its share of risks and rewards, along with the added benefits of discomfort or pleasure. It's a place of distinction. A ledge will test our mettle because we all have different tolerance levels for taking risks and wanting rewards.

In the mountains, the ledge is a dangerous place. Whether we ended up there by design or by accident, it's not always the best place to be. Said another way, there's usually not a long line waiting to go out on a ledge.

A mountain ledge has the power to take our breath away. Ledges in our personal lives can do that too. When we're out there, it makes sense to stay calm and appreciate that we haven't fallen off. While the experience can be lonely and terrifying, it can also be the most gratifying choice we've ever made.

Ledges in life can be dangerous, but they also provide unique vantage points. Whatever metaphor we use to describe our life-challenging ledges, we become stronger when we choose to overcome them rather than allowing them to hold us back.

A ledge on a mountain might be terrifying to one person and exhilarating to the next. The same holds true for real-life ledges. These are the places and situations where the circumstances are precarious and tolerance levels are tested. Suffice it to say, a ledge can have a significant impact on our lives.

Replay

- The ledge is the place where we know the risk is high and the reward may be questionable, but the position is always precarious.
- The ledge is a place of distinction.

Action to Take / Questions to Ponder

What ledges have you found in your life? Is your initial response to ledges (or risks) to avoid them, cautiously consider them, or just enjoy the view? How did you assess your response to each?

IV CAUSE AND EFFECT

Events and actions cause things to happen, and the results may be good or bad. Occasionally, we are at the mercy of those results.

INFLUENCE

People will remember that you influenced how you made them
feel, and this feeling can last a lifetime.

Our surroundings influence us. Others influence us because of things they've said or not said, or things they do or do not do. Influence occurs everywhere, all the time. The weather, the traffic, our living and working environments—all continuously influence how we think and feel.

The mountains do this as well. They sometimes influence by allowing just the right amount of moisture and cloud cover to pass over them. Said another way, the mountains act as a barrier to many storms approaching the Front Range and especially the Denver area.

External events influence our lives similarly. If you notice your mood has changed suddenly, try asking, "What's influenced my mood? I didn't feel this way earlier." You may find what has triggered this unconscious change.

Influence can be subtle, so subtle we might not notice its effect on us and our decisions until much later. Some people, for example, try to influence with money or manipulation, but many more choose to influence for positive, less selfish reasons.

It should be obvious that the better way to influence is by example. As Gandhi said, "Be the change in the world you wish to see."

Influence by example has a powerful, longer-lasting effect because it's harder to forget the kindness you offered or the assistance you gave. People will remember that you influenced how you made them feel, and this feeling can last a lifetime.

Replay

- A better way to influence is by example.
- Influence by example has a powerful, longer-lasting effect on others.

Action to Take / Questions to Ponder

Catch yourself attempting to influence someone or something. Notice what you do differently and why in order to achieve the outcome you're looking for.

We should treat extremes as boundaries, markers that shows us
the end limits of things.

Extremes are the opposite ends of something; events,
facts, and circumstances are examples. Extremes are
neither good nor bad, but they help us determine on
which side of the fence we'd like to sit.

Consider weather extremes in the Rocky Mountains.
They are unique, and temperatures can vary widely, even
during the same day. It could be seventy-five degrees in
the afternoon in late October, but twelve hours later,
it's down in the twenties. The mountains allow these
extremes to occur.

Extremes in life occur just as randomly. Job stresses,
family pressures, deadlines, and mechanical breakdowns
all create extremes. We can ignore these situations, get
angry at them, or be afraid, but one thing we can assume:
they usually require a response from us.

Our moods, perspectives, and energy levels all affect how we respond to extremes. It's a good thing to remember this when we need to push ourselves beyond our normal limits to accomplish a big goal.

Extremes are helpful because they shed light and offer perspective. We should treat extremes as boundaries, markers that show us the end limits of things. An extreme can also act as a good roadmap or a reliable compass when we are trying to navigate a complicated situation.

Finally, extremes help us see the differences between things like good and bad, or fast and slow, which help us make decisions. When we've experienced extremes, we are better equipped to develop our perspective, recognize the differences, and make informed decisions.

Replay

- Extremes are neither good nor bad.
- Treat extremes as boundaries, markers that show us the end limits of things.

Action to Take / Questions to Ponder

How do you find extremes helpful?

We affect our environment
by putting things in motion.

Everything on earth moves. Movement = life.

Water, rocks, air, dirt, and trees all move. Even buildings and mountains move. It's beneficial to remember this because it's easy to believe we must adopt a slower existence as we get older.

Many people believe less movement is what we should practice as we age, but consider this: if life is motion, shouldn't we push harder as we get older? Even science and medicine promote more exercise and activity for older folks.

Mountain streams and waterfalls appear to move at two speeds: fast and faster. As the water moves, it rushes, splatters, and slams into rocks, fallen trees, and everything else in its path.

We, likewise, affect our environment by putting things in motion. Our movement takes many forms: actions we take or don't, apologies we offer or accept, or love we give or receive. The result of each action or inaction comes from movement, and each has a positive or negative effect.

Nearly all our well-intentioned, thoughtful actions will create a positive reaction, result, or consequence. The antithesis, or counteraction, is that careless, ill-intentioned, or evil actions tend to yield negative results.

We have no guarantee our well-intentioned actions will yield a positive result. Still, if action is a necessary part of daily life, why not choose it?

Replay

- *Nearly* all our well-intentioned, thoughtful actions will create a positive reaction, result, or consequence.
- If life is motion, shouldn't we push ourselves harder to stay in motion as we get older?

Action to Take / Questions to Ponder

Describe the kinds of motion(s) you employ to help yourself and others.

The actions we take and the things we create all leave personal footprints on people and the world around us.

After fresh snow has fallen, it's impossible not to leave footprints on a mountain trail. Footprints are personal imprints, evidence of our presence, but footprints are impermanent; they will be gone by next snowfall or the first melt.

Our lives leave footprints too, but they last much longer than footprints in new snow. The actions we take and the things we create all leave personal footprints on people and the world around us. The question is, will this impression be worthy enough to last?

Perhaps the best reason to be mindful of our footprints is that your actions are being watched by others, even if unconsciously. They are being watched, not necessarily in judgment but certainly for perspective; to compare their actions to yours.

Remembering that our footprints have long-term effects on others will help us stay grounded. Footprints have the potential to positively affect others for long periods of time. Criminals, saints, corporate thieves, and nurturing parents all leave footprints. It's our choice whose examples we'll follow.

It's a sobering thought to realize our short time on earth will likely be washed away over the evolving years. Some of us see this as an eternal sentence to obscurity, but others go out of their way to be remembered for something . . . even if it's something bad.

So instead of becoming melancholy about our eventual obscurity, I suggest you use your time wisely by seeking to make an imprint on the world to make it better, even in a small way! This needn't be a self-aggrandizing choice. You can do it one action at a time, one person at a time.

If you choose to help just one person in a meaningful way, you will have left a footprint that could be payed forward in ways you may never know.

One thing is certain: if you do nothing, you are guaranteed to leave no footprints.

Replay

- Our lives leave footprints, and they last much longer than footprints in new snow.
- If you do nothing, you are guaranteed to leave no footprints.

Action to Take / Questions to Ponder

In what ways could you leave footprints for others to follow by your helpfulness or attentiveness?

V | RESPONSIVENESS

Things happen; we respond . . . or not.

We don't ascend a mountain or climb above life's challenges by accident.

Going up a mountain is usually more difficult than traveling down one. Granted, this is not a big revelation.

We move uphill at a slow, deliberate pace, which allows us to walk, run, bike, or drive in a predictable manner. When we climb uphill, we encounter the same twists and turns as going down, but we require more power and effort. Not only does it take strength to go uphill but also persistence; both are necessary resources when ascending a mountain.

Going uphill is a metaphor most people understand right away. We don't ascend a mountain or climb above life's challenges by accident.

The same skills and capabilities needed for a mountain ascent are needed when we encounter life's big hills. It's those twists, turns, bumps, and setbacks that make life interesting and challenging.

And, likewise, sheer persistence will not get us up the hill without strength. One way or another, we must access the energy and the drive inside us to keep moving upwards. Such an effort may sound demanding, but facing challenges head-on is a habit that helps us throughout our lives.

Those two ingredients are necessary as well when we encounter life's battles. As the metaphor "uphill battle" suggests, we shouldn't expect the journey to the top to be easy; few uphill journeys are.

Knowing when it's time to summon our internal power will help us ascend with confidence, whether we're addressing a life challenge or ascending a mountain trail.

Replay

- Sheer persistence will not get us up the hill without strength.
- The same skills and capabilities needed for a mountain ascent are needed when we encounter life's big hills.

Action to Take / Questions to Ponder

Imagine and/or define what your best response might be (or has been) to one of life's big challenges.

There will always be slippery patches around us, but it's one thing to take calculated risks and another to be reckless.

As a lifelong runner, I ran the streets of South Florida for thirty years. The roads were endlessly flat. The only inclines were the bridges going over the Intracoastal Waterway or old landfills that had been turned into parks. Talk about contrasts in sights and smells.

The Rocky Mountains are different from South Florida in obvious ways.

One quiet Saturday morning in early December, I went for a run. The snow fell gently to the ground. It was neither snowflakes nor ice crystals; it was something in between, falling to earth like tiny white crumbs from the sky. They were in ample quantity to cover the ground and deaden the street sounds. I began to drift off into a meditative state.

Coming down a gently rolling hill, I spotted a patch of ice a few feet ahead of me. There was no avoiding it. I couldn't stop, slow down, or turn away. I was committed. I faced a moment of truth. I did have some options. I could drop lower to the ground in a controlled fall, I could decrease the stride of my last step to control my center of gravity, or I could just keep going and hope I did not fall.

In life, we have several metaphors for these kinds of situations: a rough patch, a curve ball, an unexpected twist, or a stroke of bad luck. We've all experienced them.

We live in an age when reputations, built over years, can be lost in minutes because of an impulsive social media post. So resolve to start making better decisions right now.

There will always be slippery patches around us. Sometimes the best we can do is to resolve to make better decisions in the future to reduce the chances of slipping. We might occasionally have to learn a lesson the hard way, but try not to let it be from a cavalier decision.

On that quiet snowy day, I slowed and lowered myself to the ground, but I still fell on my butt.

Replay

- We live in an age when reputations, built over years, can be lost in minutes because of an impulsive social media post.
- Sometimes the best we can do is to resolve to make better decisions in the future to reduce the chances of slipping.

Action to Take / Questions to Ponder

In what areas of your life are you most prone to your own slipping and sliding?

All of us go through life adapting to change; it's a condition of living, surviving, and thriving.

Plants and wildlife in the mountains are capable of living in the harshest of conditions (think evergreens and longhorn sheep). There is a highly active but small animal who lives in the mountains named the pika. It lives in the severe winter conditions of the mountains, where other animals typically stay away from.

The pika lives above the timberline and does not hibernate during winter. Instead, it spends much of its time eating the large stores of vegetation it has strategically gathered for the long, cold mountain winter.

Just as the pika has adapted to its environment, people adapt and adjust in similar ways.

For example, people don't go hiking in the mountains with the intention of not surviving. We are planning to survive before we take our first step onto the trail. We prepare in order to adapt to possible challenges, so we plan, pack, and act with the intention of enjoying the trip and returning safely.

All of us go through life adapting to change; it's a condition of living and thriving, and sometimes surviving. Adapting to change requires a conscious effort on our part to consider all variables while zeroing in on the most advantageous response we can take.

We mostly make adaptive choices for practical reasons: climate preferences, family reasons, job opportunities, and partnership decisions.

Adapting is a life skill as much as it is a survival tactic. We employ it as needed to effectively confront life's challenging circumstances. A thoughtful adaptive response gives us a better opportunity to succeed no matter where we live or what we do.

Replay

- People don't go hiking in the mountains with the intention of not surviving.
- Adapting to change is a condition of living and thriving, and sometimes surviving.

Action to Take / Questions to Ponder

Rate yourself on a scale of 1 to 10 (10 being the best) on your ability to adapt. What could you start or stop doing that would improve your ability to more comfortably adapt to change?

DESCENDING

21

Going downhill demands increased focus, control, and balance.
There's more going on here than meets the eye.

There are few things more exhilarating than descending a mountain road or trail on a bright, clear summer day. (Some would counter that a brilliant, cold winter day is just as exhilarating.)

Those accustomed to downhill mountain driving know it's best to drop down to a lower gear and let the car's transmission control the speed. Braking continuously might cause the car to skid or the brakes to wear out.

Going uphill may require more effort, but going downhill demands increased focus, control, and balance. All three play major roles in our ability to arrive safely at the bottom.

On a mountain road, going downhill demands a safe speed to competently navigate the challenging

87

twists and turns. Like our own private video game, we negotiate the obstacles in front of us while keeping a steady eye towards the distance.

A life challenge may occasionally feel like a steep mountain-road descent. A steady eye is needed here too. Here we operate in a multiplex mode. We are conscious of the present, we anticipate what might happen next, and we reflect upon our knowledge and experience. Problems can arise if we place more emphasis on the future and not enough on the present or vice versa.

The art of being present means we are fully aware of the present while being mindful of the past and being prepared for the future. This balance helps us navigate life more competently.

Yes, going uphill is more physically demanding, but remember, moving downhill in life and on a mountain road requires focus, balance, and care. There's more going on here than meets the eye.

Replay

- Going downhill demands increased focus, control, and balance.
- The art of being present means we are fully aware of the present while being mindful of the past and prepared for the future.

Action to Take / Questions to Ponder

When do you find yourself in downhill life situations? How do you prepare for them?

RESPONDING

22

*When we respond, we are still emotional, but our emotion
is tempered.*

Wе all need reminding about the importance of
being prepared. We can't respond effectively if
we're not properly prepared.

In the mountains, being prepared is essential because
the mountains present a unique set of challenges. The
possibilities are numerous—rain, hail, snow, wild
animals, lightning, blocked trails and roads—but at the
top of the list is getting lost. While the list of challenges
is long, the consequences of inadequate preparation are
even longer and more daunting.

Good preparation enables us to enjoy and safely
survive our excursions in life, but it also allows us to
competently respond to life's challenging situations.

Preparation and responding complement each
other, and the glue holding them together is called

practice. Obviously, we can't anticipate every possible scenario, so learning how to stay calm in unexpected situations is a good thing to practice. Through practice, our most thoughtful and effective actions will originate from our ability to *respond* instead of react.

When we react, we are driven more by emotion, such as fear, shock, or anger. When reacting, our actions tend to be without thought or regard for consequences.

Responding is more effective. When we respond, we are still emotional, but our emotion is tempered by a keen eye towards the longer-term, positive outcome. The common expression *cooler heads will prevail* recognizes that a less emotionally driven person will prevail better than someone who simply reacts out of emotion.

A more effective way to learn how to respond well is to practice "not reacting." That is, when you catch yourself being surprised by circumstances . . . slow down. Don't let your emotions take over automatically. (*Note:* A little discernment is required here. If a truck is bearing down on you and you're on the sidewalk—react! Run! Just confirm you're not about to run into traffic.)

If we can anchor in our brains that responding is always more effective than reacting, we'll be in a slightly better position for the unexpected.

Replay

- Preparation and responding complement each other, and the glue holding them together is called practice.
- Our most thoughtful and effective actions will originate from our ability to *respond* instead of react.

Action to Take / Questions to Ponder

How do preparation and practice help you respond more effectively?

VI | AWARENESS

Awareness is a choice, a choice that enhances life, helps us appreciate what we have, and prepares us to be ready to assist others. It is a core skill we all need.

Air centers us;
it brings us back to the essence of life.

The air is thinner in the mountains.

Some people may notice it by their shortness of breath or their general feeling of nausea when they first arrive here. Those feelings usually go away after a few days once their bodies adjust to the lower oxygen levels.

This acclimation takes place without conscious effort on our part. Our bodies adapt, and then one day we notice we aren't having trouble breathing at five thousand feet anymore. We all take our body's ability to adjust itself for granted.

Food, water, and shelter are the necessities of life we most need. When these needs are satisfied, we don't give them a second thought. We tend to take other things for granted, too, like our five senses and our ability to think, move our muscles, and breathe. These are daily miracles, yet we sometimes fail to recognize them as such.

The simple act of breathing, for example, easily slips our notice, yet we take on average about twenty-three thousand breaths a day.

In the mountains, at sea level, and in between, air is the simplest, most immediate need we have. We immediately appreciate air when it is absent.

Air centers us; it brings us back to the essence of life. By consciously taking a deep breath, we become aware of its presence. When we consciously breathe, we recognize we are doing something vital to our existence. Once we stop breathing, our bodies begin screaming for air.

When atop a fourteen-thousand-foot mountain, there is even less oxygen. We won't pass out and most of us will not be harmed, but we will notice a change in our breathing capabilities as our bodies attempt to adjust to the scarcity. As we descend to lower altitudes, we more fully appreciate the air . . . and the fact we can breathe at all. And then we forget. It's a curious cycle we go through.

Being aware of your ability to breathe won't change your life, but it can deepen your appreciation of life in general . . . and that's a good thing.

Replay

- There are many life-giving daily miracles we fail to recognize or appreciate.
- When we consciously breathe, we recognize we are doing something vital to our existence.

Action to Take / Questions to Ponder

What daily life-giving miracles can you quietly begin to appreciate more often?

The significance of a mountain or a cathedral can be measured by the feelings it evokes in us.

It's easy to feel we're in a special place when standing atop of one of Colorado's fourteeners. The enormity and breadth remind us that we are in a remarkable location, atop an amazing perch on one of God's cathedrals.

Over the centuries, billions of dollars and millions of lives (artisans, masons, sculptors, carpenters) have been dedicated to building churches that reach to the heavens, all to enhance the impression we are closer to God. In the spiritual sense, many people recognize they are as close to God as they want to be, whether they're on Pikes Peak or in the Cathedral of Notre-Dame.

The significance of a mountain or a cathedral can be measured by the feelings it evokes in us. We may not feel spiritual while ascending a mountain, but we'll likely feel different when we get to the top. We may feel different for only a moment or two; then our attention shifts elsewhere. But the sights and sounds of the mountain will always remind us we're in a distinctively different place.

Most people living in or near the mountains realize their significant, positive influence. The residents are far from indifferent to their locale. In fact, they are inspired by it. This doesn't make them any better, smarter, or faster than the rest of us, but they are more consciously upbeat and genuinely jazzed by living in an exceptional part of the country.

In the mountains, we can say we are higher in the sky than others. We're also a little nearer to the sun, and perhaps just a bit closer to God . . . without the church.

Replay

- The enormity and breadth of a Colorado fourteener remind us that we are in a remarkable location, atop an amazing perch on one of God's cathedrals.
- People living in the mountains are consciously upbeat and genuinely jazzed by living in an exceptional part of the country.

Action or Question

When was the last time you were inspired or excited about a location you lived in or visited?

Magnificence goes beyond landscapes and buildings. It is as fundamental as doing a good deed for a stranger for no other reason than to help.

The Rocky Mountains of Colorado have a magnificence about them that is second to none. Whether you're seeing them for the first time or the one-hundredth, they stand as imposing land masses, emerging from the ground and reaching for the heavens. Now, here's the big leap: people can be this way too.

We may not reach heights of fourteen thousand feet, and we may rarely evoke feelings of awe and wonder, but on an average day, we have the ability to do wondrous things that may seem magnificent to others. That analogy isn't made to exaggerate or impress but to illustrate how we often fail to see how amazing we really are or can be.

We don't always recognize how special life is. Some people feel their lives are cursed, and others may believe they've been dealt a bad hand. The other path to take is the simple act of looking for what's good in life, especially what is magnificent, which increases our ability to see it in the first place.

Magnificence, like beauty, is in the eye of the beholder. As with our outlook on life, we can choose to see problems, or we can actively seek the magnificence surrounding us every day.

We may choose not to be impressed by the same snow-covered mountains we see every day, or we can deliberately take notice of the mountains' unique contours and colors and be awed by the sight. Likewise, we can walk along the street and notice litter, noise, and traffic, or we can look around and be impressed by the enormity and magnificence of the massive manmade structures surrounding us.

Magnificence goes beyond landscapes and buildings. It is as fundamental as doing a good deed for a stranger for no other reason than to help. Magnificence is doing something small or grand, like giving or sharing an item you value, because you wanted to do so. There are a million ways to allow magnificence into your life and to see it in other people.

Magnificence is not something to be leveraged or used to score points. It's not intended to be showy. The more we encourage it and seek it, the more it's likely to become an everyday occurrence. Wouldn't it be amazing if magnificence were an everyday event that was the norm instead of the exception? We can make magnificence happen if we consciously look for it in others and manifest it in ourselves.

Replay

- The simple act of looking for what's good in life, especially what is magnificent, increases our ability to see it in the first place.
- Magnificence, like beauty, is in the eye of the beholder; we can choose to see problems, or we can actively seek the magnificence surrounding us every day.

Action to Take / Questions to Ponder

What's magnificent about you and about the people around you?

Lookouts play a vital role for us because we can't spot all the hazards in life.

D evil's Head Fire Lookout Station is a one-hour, thirty-nine-mile drive from Denver. At 9,748 feet in elevation, it is the only lookout station in Colorado staffed by the National Forest Service.

The lookout's original structure was built in 1912, and the present building was constructed in 1951. The lookout offers a 360-degree, one-hundred-mile panoramic view. The lookout helps rangers spot and communicate the locations of forest fires to ground forces.

In daily life, a lookout is like a guardian angel, someone there for us when we need warning of things we should avoid or be aware of.

Most of us have had lookouts in our lives before, not just for dangerous situations but also for the day-to-day, seemingly inconsequential events we often miss but shouldn't.

Lookouts can be friends, relatives, or complete strangers. They play a vital role for us because we can't spot all the hazards in life. Lookouts also point out the joyful moments too.

Don't forget, it's equally important to be someone else's lookout. It's always great to receive help. The next time you see an opportunity to be a lookout for someone else, remember how it felt to be helped by your lookout.

The need for a lookout never goes away, in life or in the mountains. Recognize a lookout's significance in your life and stay alert for opportunities to be someone else's lookout too.

Replay

- A lookout is like a guardian angel, someone there for us when we need warning of things we should avoid or be aware of.
- It's equally important to be someone else's lookout.

Action to Take / Questions to Ponder

When was the last time a lookout helped you?
When was the last time you become a lookout for
someone else?

GUARDRAILS

There aren't always guardrails in life to protect us from our mistakes and bad choices.

Ever see those padded rails along the sides of a bowling lane that keep the ball from dropping into the gutter? They're mostly there for kids, but adults rely on them when they are learning the game. A bowling alley doesn't offer much forgiveness; if your ball falls in the gutter, it will never strike a pin.

Shifting focus to the mountains, consider those winding, two-lane mountain roads where there's only enough pavement for two cars to drive in opposite directions. The lanes are small, with no shoulders and no guardrails to prevent either driver from going over the edge. There are not many roads like this, but many people who travel upon them sometimes come away from the experience quite shaken.

In daily life, guardrails take different forms. During childhood, for example, you may have slept on the top mattress of a bunk bed with guardrails to keep you from rolling out of bed in the middle of the night and plummeting to the floor.

There aren't always guardrails in life to protect us from our mistakes and bad choices. Beyond the protective structures that exist in life—warning signs, alarms, and "undo" keys—the best protection we have for living without guardrails is staying aware.

Awareness won't always prevent us from crashing, but it helps keep us a little more conscious of what we are doing, especially in dangerous situations. Here's the thing: despite the danger of moving about in dangerous settings without guardrails, there are some people who will act without regard to the possible consequences. For example, does texting while driving a mountain road without guardrails sound like an intelligent decision to you?

The harsh reality is that when taking chances, even with guardrails, the likelihood of a negative result increases. Our best choice, especially if we're inclined to take chances, is to ramp up our awareness level, to be more mindful and more careful, and to focus on being totally present.

Guardrails will not always protect you . . . unless you're bowling.

Replay

- The best protection we have for living without guardrails is staying aware.
- The harsh reality of taking risky chances, even with guardrails, is that it increases the possibility of a negative result.

Action to Take / Questions to Ponder

Where are you playing it too safe in your life and using guardrails to insulate you?

VII | PREPARATION

Preparation is a state of constant practicing.
Knowing how to prepare is a critical life skill
that serves us in so many ways.

We do have an amazing capacity to adapt, but our success at adapting is directly related to our ability to anticipate change.

In the mountains, change is constant and universal. Weather, terrain, and plant and animal life all change there.

A way to experience that mountain change is by traveling to the top of Pikes Peak on a hot summer day. Temperatures start in the eighties at the base, and people usually dress in shorts and t-shirts.

As you ascend, an abundance of greenery—shrubs, trees, and evergreens—dominates the landscape. Before long, plant life begins thinning out as you now feel fall-like temperatures. You may find yourself putting on a sweater.

Though the sun still shines brightly, the air is much cooler and thinner. As you approach the top, you pass the timberline. There, the only plant life remaining is alpine grasses, mountain flowers, and the random bristlecone pines scattered around the moonlike terrain.

At the top, the change is even more radical. It's thirty to forty-five degrees cooler, and there is a brisk wind. The only way to enjoy the visit is to wear the warmer clothing you brought along.

Everyday life isn't much different. Handling life's changes may not always be as simple as putting on a sweater, but learning to anticipate life's variables assists us with adapting to the more common challenges in life. New jobs, partners, or residences are typical kinds of changes we sometimes handle.

Not surprisingly, most of us struggle with change, and oftentimes we go out of our way to avoid it.

We have an amazing capacity to adapt, but our success at adapting is directly related to our ability to anticipate change. It's also easy to overlook the obvious preventive step: preparation.

Preparation won't guarantee avoidance of change that comes our way, but it does increase the odds we will adapt to it more effectively.

Change is life's moving target, although sometimes it may feel like change is the arrow and we are the target.

Replay

- Preparation won't guarantee avoidance of change that comes our way, but it does increase the odds we will adapt to it more effectively.
- Not surprisingly, most of us struggle with change, and oftentimes we go out of our way to avoid it.

Action to Take / Questions to Ponder

What is your best recipe for anticipating and handling change?

Trailblazing is a mindset.

Not everyone wants to be first. For many, going first means a departure from a predictable life of comfort and safety. A predictable life involves little or no risk, which is why lots of people choose it.

In the mountains, most people follow established or marked trails when they go hiking. It's the smart and safe thing to do. Here, predictability is highly attractive; it means knowing where the trail is.

Trailblazing, on the other hand, deliberately involves more risk. It's not as risky as rock climbing, but it will test our wits, push us out of our comfort zone, and require us to leave the traditional path.

In life, we tend to choose known paths because of their predictability. We'll wear the same clothes, eat the same foods, drive the same roads to work, perform repetitive work, and try to maintain predictable relationships because we don't want surprises. This isn't criticism; it's just to highlight how much repetition factors into our lives.

To trailblaze in the mountains means we expect to get lost once in a while. We want to avoid getting lost (so we bring a map or GPS) and not having enough food, water, or proper clothing (so we bring those too) to make it through a cold night in the mountains.

In life, it's very similar. For those who find themselves bored or looking for more in life, choosing an unpredictable path may reduce feelings of monotony. In today's world, trailblazing might simply mean turning off our GPS when we travel an unfamiliar road. Most of us, however, choose not to do this because we're in a hurry or we prefer the more predictable path.

Trailblazing is a mindset. It's a choice we make to live our lives less predictably, not by living on the edge but by mixing things up occasionally. We don't always need all the answers to get started or to keep going.

Replay

- To trailblaze in the mountains means we expect to get lost once in a while; it's very similar in life.

- Choosing an unpredictable path may reduce feelings of monotony.

Action to Take / Questions to Ponder

What would we do if we weren't in a hurry? Do you follow predictable paths and habits, or do you trailblaze occasionally? Experiment!

An imagined storm (or problem) can feel as bad as a real one.

Billions of dollars are spent each year for meteorologists to predict the weather. Sometimes weather forecasters get it right, but other times they are so wrong it seems they've deliberately fabricated a prediction to annoy us.

In the mountains, it is harder to predict the weather, especially the formation of storms. Air masses, which are made of moisture and contrasting temperatures, tend to clash in unpredictable ways when they cross the high peaks of the Rockies.

Regardless of the complexities of predicting a mountain storm, it's still an easier task than guessing how people will respond to difficult situations or personal storms, as we'll call them.

Said another way, human behavior is more fickle than a storm front crossing the Continental Divide. And yet we still expect people, ourselves included, to act in a predictable manner, as if there exists some ancient text summarizing the behavioral responses people will make in given situations.

The reality is that life is as unpredictable as the weather. It is essential we understand this if we want to endure the storms that will occur in our lives.

To complicate things further, we are masters at imagining and worrying about every potential problem or storm that could occur in our lives, even if there's really little chance they could happen. We imagine these storms so well, we allow fear, dread, and worry into our lives. An imagined storm (or problem) can feel as bad as a real one.

We all hit rough patches in life. Whether we call them storms, challenges, problems, or crises, when they occur, they usually require us to respond, even if that means doing nothing.

The preparation for life's storms is to apply a bit of prethought about how we might handle the occasional surprise storm. We need not go through life carrying an umbrella everywhere, but we shouldn't be foolish enough to think the sun is going to shine every day either.

Storms happen, but it's reassuring to know that all storms pass.

Replay

- Life is as unpredictable as the weather.
- We need not go through life carrying an umbrella everywhere, but we shouldn't be foolish enough to think the sun is going to shine every day either.

Action to Take / Questions to Ponder

Describe your best and worst responses to two personal storms you've experienced.

*When we do feel overwhelmed, the best question to ask
ourselves is, "What are my options here?"*

To overwhelm something or someone involves power and energy. Overwhelm can happen in the mountains as easily as during a walk through town. We all will feel overwhelmed from time to time in our lives.

On a peaceful mountaintop, a violent summer storm can form in minutes. One moment it's sunny and hot; the next moment it looks like the world is about to end. Storms appear in our personal lives in a similar fashion. We call them *personal storms*, arriving as suddenly and unexpectedly as a thunderstorm.

Storms are obvious triggers for feeling overwhelmed.

When hikers are surprised by an abrupt storm, they may immediately seek lower ground. But the intensity of the storm could also cause them to panic. It's not hard to imagine what panic looks like during a sudden violent storm at the top of a mountain. When we encounter personal storms, they usually require us to think fast and act quickly.

When faced with a sudden personal storm, it's easy to panic.

It's essential to get our feelings in check when we feel overwhelmed. Obviously, this is easier said than done. When we do feel overwhelmed, the best question to ask ourselves is, "What are my options here?"

The point is to recognize that we all will face overwhelming obstacles and challenges from time to time. Actively searching for options helps us to shift away from emotion and force some logical thinking to take place.

Replay

- Storms are obvious triggers for feeling overwhelmed.
- It's essential to get our feelings in check when we feel overwhelmed.

Action to Take / Questions to Ponder

How do you typically respond when you experience the feeling of being overwhelmed? Do you panic or try to reflect before taking action? Could you/should you slow down your response time for a few seconds' additional reflection?

*Responding capably to disorientation in life
is critical.*

Mountains don't get lost; people do.

While that sounds clear and simple, here's what isn't: the number of people who get lost in the mountains every year. It's true; it can be difficult to navigate a multidimensional incline containing vast amounts of trees, shrubs, and boulders, so it's easy to see why people get disoriented. It only makes sense for people to prepare for a trip into the mountains so they can avoid getting lost. But here's the thing: despite our best preparations, we can still get lost.

We all tend to drift off course once in a while. It can happen both in the mountains and in everyday life. Responding capably to disorientation in life is critical. Do we overreact, or do we remain calm? Do we jump to a conclusion, or do we think things through as quickly as we can?

Each of us will occasionally feel disoriented in life. We may feel hopeless, frustrated, or even adrift, believing we're powerless to adapt, but adaptation is what we must seek.

We make mistakes when we are lost or disoriented. Sometimes we panic; other times we remain inactive. We may try pretending nothing is wrong, and we start making poor decisions.

As noted in a previous chapter, knowing how to respond well versus simply reacting to unexpected situations is a serious life skill. Responding capably can mean the difference between life and death in the mountains when you're disoriented. In everyday life, it can be the difference between success and failure.

Responding eats reacting for breakfast every time.

Replay

- Despite our best preparations, we can still get lost.
- Responding capably can mean the difference between life and death in the mountains when you're disoriented.

Action to Take / Questions to Ponder

Do you have a process to prevent yourself from becoming disoriented during stressful times?

VIII | PURPOSE

We all have a purpose in life.
Some of us are more aware of it than others
and respond to it.

We have our own timberline, a line in our lives we have chosen
to protect ourselves from the noise, intrusions, and interference
of people or situations.

Crossing the timberline of a mountain means
you have passed into an area where most plant
life cannot survive because of the altitude. When
approaching the timberline, usually around twelve
thousand feet, you'll see that the scenery changes from
thick stands of pines to scattered shrubs, dirt, and rocks
in a matter of a few hundred feet.

The starkness of the land above the timberline
conveys desolation, yet the barrenness of the landscape
is still breathtaking. On a mountaintop, boundaries are
revealed—up here, barrenness; below, vegetation.

Shifting to everyday life, we have our own timberline,
if you will—a boundary line. This line represents the
places in our lives where we have chosen to protect

ourselves from the noise, intrusion, and interference of people or situations.

This boundary also include lines we absolutely will not cross, places we will never allow ourselves to go, and people we unconditionally refuse to let into our lives.

We establish these boundaries to protect ourselves. The key to success with personal boundaries is to remind ourselves occasionally why we established that boundary in the first place, such as a situation being too uncomfortable or a person being toxic.

The good news is that once we establish a boundary line, we mostly will automatically enforce it.

Replay

- Boundary lines include lines we absolutely will not cross, places we will never allow ourselves to go, and people we unconditionally refuse to let into our lives.
- We establish these boundaries to protect ourselves.

Action to Take / Questions to Ponder

Have you set boundaries in your life? How have they helped or protected you from people and circumstances you did not want in your life? What additional boundaries do you need? Are there any boundaries you need to adjust?

*Go ahead and enjoy the view, and experience a way of life
many people just dream about.*

Silly or not, there are inhabitants of the lower
elevations of the United States who believe people
living and playing in the mountains are foolish. This
belief stems from the conventional myths in existence
for generations about how extremes in altitude, cold
weather, and thinness of the air are all detrimental
to our health. These factors sway people away from
the mountains

It's a fair guess that many people reading this find
the mountains attractive. And it's also safe to say these
people really don't care what others think; they are
having too much fun enjoying life in the mountains.
If you feel you're a member of this foolish group, you
probably see the importance of ignoring the "madding
crowd" and doing what you feel is right for you.

As long as you put no one else at risk, including those who have to rescue you because you've been careless, you are perfectly entitled to happily enduring the challenges of the mountains. So go ahead and enjoy the view, and experience a way of life many people just dream about.

Like mountains, people can rise above the fray and not be affected by what others say and do. It's important to respect your own thoughts and feelings; they can insulate you from wanting or needing the approval of others.

It's a universal urge to want acceptance and to be liked by others. Spending too much time chasing their approval is as foolish as it is futile. It's better to focus on our goals and reduce our tendency to be influenced by others.

Unfortunately, many of us fail to realize this early enough in life. We waste time chasing approval instead of focusing on our goals and aspirations. Focusing on our goals reduces our tendency to be unduly influenced by the opinions of others.

We all look foolish occasionally; this is a near certainty in life. Either we handle being foolish with grace, or we feel bad and worry until it happens again.

Replay

- It's a universal urge to want acceptance and to be liked by others.
- We can all rise above the fray and not be affected by what others say and do.

Action to Take / Questions to Ponder

Think about one time when you felt you were foolish. Did it bother you? How much? Why?

People, whether in teams, organizations, or families, always accomplish more together.

People unite for many reasons—work, parties, weddings, concerts, and meetings. The list is endless. There are also naturally occurring events and attractions that bring people together. A mountain is one of those attractions, just like a meteor shower, the northern lights, or giant waves crashing on the beach.

Water is a people magnet in its many forms too: lakes, streams, and waterfalls.

Water, mountain-sourced or not, gives and attracts life. Like prospectors of the Gold Rush days who sought gold and followed a creek towards the mountains, today's travelers are pursuing similar benefits at the water's edge but in running shoes and on bikes. The riches now are better health and an active lifestyle.

Water has always brought people together. The city of Denver started near the confluence of Cherry Creek and the Platte River. Today, these waters course through the city towards what is known as Confluence Park, where walking and biking trails run parallel to the flowing waters and unite people from all walks of life.

We all consciously bring people together for a variety of reasons. We create gatherings to unite them for a cause, for a higher purpose.

Rivers and streams run naturally, unerringly towards the ocean. We, too, should move naturally and unerringly when we unite for a higher purpose. It needn't be a let's-change-the-world kind of purpose, but a *let's-make-things-better* kind isn't a bad start.

People, whether in teams, organizations, or families, always accomplish more together. A team that is united recognizes they are more than the sum of its individual parts. Uniting is also about the collaborative win and establishing higher standards for ourselves. It represents inclusiveness in the best sense of the word.

The higher purpose, whether we're in the mountains or on the street, is to come together and enjoy each other's company, working together to accomplish more while enjoying the experience.

Replay

- Ideally we create gatherings to unite people for a cause, for a higher purpose.
- Uniting is also about the collaborative win and establishing higher standards for ourselves.

Action to Take / Questions to Ponder

Name two higher purposes for which you could bring people together.

First tracks is a whimsical concept with serious connotations—
serious as in serious fun,

D eep within us is the urge to be first . . . not
necessarily to win or to beat someone in a contest,
but to lay claim to having attained something no one else
has regardless of the size of the claim. *First tracks*, for our
purposes, refers to what some people seek to accomplish
after a new snowfall.

This is no trivial point.

In the mountains, after a fresh snowfall, people have a
natural urge to leave first tracks by skiing, snowboarding,
or snowshoeing in the fresh powder. First tracks is a
whimsical concept with serious connotations—serious
as in serious fun, as Coloradans intending to be first
usually do so for temporary bragging rights. No one gets
hurt, and it's healthy competition.

This isn't the case in everyday life, unfortunately. The need and drive to be first sometimes throws a spotlight on the less-than-admirable side of some people . . . you know, the ones who go out of their way to cut in line or take something they shouldn't. These transgressions aren't criminal offenses, but they reflect the selfish, sometimes hurtful side of people.

These examples are certainly not high personal standards by which to measure ourselves, but we've all been guilty of these behaviors on occasion.

A good approach for curtailing the me-first, you-last impulse is to stop taking yourself so seriously. That brings us back to first tracks and the desire to have fun. In other words, practice lightening up a little more, and go out and make some first tracks using your creative abilities versus applying a conquer-and-consume mentality that a small percentage of people do.

First tracks means having fun but not at the expense of others.

Replay

- A good approach for curtailing the me-first, you-last impulse is to stop taking yourself so seriously.

- The need and drive to be first sometimes throws a spotlight on the less-than-admirable side of some people.

Action to Take / Questions to Ponder

What kinds of things can you do to lay some first tracks of your own just for the fun of it?

The people of Colorado are distinctly different, but they don't talk about it. They live their code through their actions.

Mountain life has its own code. The code isn't documented anywhere and you can't search for it on the internet, but people living in the mountains live by it daily. The code is a way of life outsiders don't initially understand. Like a private club with a secret handshake, mountain residents instinctively know *how* they live is as critical as *where* they live.

To test this code, once you're inside any Front Range town's city limits, step into a crosswalk with cars coming and see them stop immediately. Try entering an elevator and notice how easily a stranger strikes up a conversation with you. Changing lanes in traffic is tricky, but see what happens when you put on your blinker and easily slide into another lane on a Colorado interstate.

The unwritten code, as demonstrated above, seems to be *acknowledge and appreciate others*.

But the code isn't a code at all; it's mostly pride, pride in where they come from and who they are. And this pride seems to emerge from a concern for others, a commitment to build a better community, and an intention to be helpful to everyone. All these values are rolled into this way of life—a mountain life. These values are expressed as one spirit, or one code, belonging to the people here, who are willing to share it with you even though you're a visitor.

It's hard to define, but it seems there is a comfort level, an acceptance of things as they are, that dominates the mindset of the people who live here. Yes, people are laid back in the mountains, but they're as serious and resolute about maintaining this way of life as anyone anywhere else.

Like the habit of paying it forward, the people of Colorado are distinctly different, but they don't talk about it. They live their code through their actions.

Replay

- The code isn't a code at all; it's mostly pride, pride in where they come from and who they are.

- There is a comfort level, an acceptance of things as they are, that dominates the mindset of the people who live in Colorado.

Action to Take / Questions to Ponder

What values or code do you embrace in your life and share in your daily actions?

Longevity is about legacy and the desire to leave things better than we found them.

On occasion, people may reflect on a desire to live forever. They know it's not possible, but it's a fun exercise for the imagination. The exercise can be a starting point for us to choose to live our lives with the intention of sticking around as long as we can.

The mountains are obvious symbols of longevity. Throughout history, mountains have inspired us to do more and to be more, to not only stand out but to stick around for a while. This type of inspiration ultimately becomes a goal or intention, which helps turn our thoughts into action. This is where longevity comes in.

In the Colorado mountains, the bristlecone pine tree is a symbol of longevity. The bristlecone pine manages to survive quite well in extreme conditions. Cold temperatures, high winds, and dry soil all contribute to the tree's slow but consistent growth. The tree's resilience is evident in a handful of those trees over two thousand years old right here in Colorado. Certainly the intention to stick around is genetically embedded in these pines.

For people, longevity is both an intention and a commitment. Longevity is about legacy and our desire to leave things better than we found them. With this kind of intention, our legacy then becomes our own personal mountain.

The wish to live forever isn't at issue; the issue is your desire to stick around for as long as possible. To live a long and happy life, in my experience, is to stay mindful of what you think, do, and say. And living your life in a consistently balanced way provides a smoother road to travel in life.

Replay

- For people, longevity is both an intention and a commitment.
- The best approach is to stay mindful of what you think, do, and say.

Action to Take / Questions to Ponder

What is your intention for sticking around as long as you can?

My purpose in writing *Mountain Life* was to accentuate how much our environment positively or negatively affects us.

If we all created a list of people, places, and things that inspire us, and another list of who or what slows us down, then the secret to staying positive is to spend more time with who or what is on your first list and avoid the people and places on the second.

You might be thinking, "If life could only be as simple as making a list and paying attention to it." Well, it can be! When we're mindful of our preferences, it's amazing how much simpler life can feel.

When people work with a life coach for personal or professional growth, one of the first homework assignments they may be given is to consciously spend more time with people who give them energy, those who make them feel good. To do this means we must first discover who those energy-providers are.

The same approach works for our environment. For some people it's the mountains, for others it's the ocean, and another group might yearn for the hustle and bustle of a metropolis like New York City.

The mountains and the people who live here turned out to be the energy-givers for me. Of all the places I've lived in or visited, no other area has so positively affected my life as Colorado's Front Range. It's that good!

A basic theme throughout *Mountain Life* is "*Be engaged with life*" ... which is another way of saying, "Be present." We all have periods during our day when we live by remote control. We do our work, we respond to questions, and we go to lunch or dinner with others, yet somewhere in those periods, we may disconnect.

We might be thinking about a deadline at work, bringing our car in for service, or wondering what we'll do this weekend. But as you know, they're all mind games distracting us from being fully engaged with life in the present.

Don't misunderstand. We all do it. We must do it . . . sometimes. But if your modus operandi is to be constantly distracted—thinking, reading, listening to music, playing video games—life is passing you by.

The secret, as with most things in life, is balance. Yes, let your mind wander, read books, listen to music, watch television, and play video games, but don't forget to reengage with life in the present frequently.

So as you close this book, consider starting each day *being more prepared*. Whether you're mountain hiking or shopping for groceries, nothing beats a rough plan for your day.

And as you hike or shop, make sure you *take time to appreciate what is right in front of you*. It might be the amazing view from up above or simply the variety of items on the store shelf. The act of acknowledging and appreciating will uplift you.

And last, *stay aware*. Obviously, it's as important to stay on the trail while hiking as it is to get off at the right subway stop. The only way this happens is if you remain aware.

Go ahead—take a deep breath, explore, question, run, hike, bike, move your body, exercise your mind, and consciously and constantly seek full engagement with the people, places, and things that surround you. What you will find is that a mountain life can be lived as easily by the ocean, in the Great Plains, or in a big city as it truly is in the mountains.

ACKNOWLEDGEMENTS

Thanking people on paper is not nearly as impactful as expressing your feelings in person. I intend to do so before they read these words.

Since my arrival in Colorado three years ago, I have met many individuals who've realigned my perception and belief that people can be more than just civilized with one another and actually be helpful and caring.

A number of people have gone out of their way to help me get oriented to my new home state.

In no particular order, I would like to extend my sincere thanks to the following Coloradans:

Colin Kresock, John Brackney, Britt Benton, Jennifer Folaron, David Johnson, Eric Adams, John Wilson, Steve Lente, David Mead, Bill Shepard, and Kathleen Quinn Votaw.

All of these people freely offered me their time, talent, and insight, and I am forever indebted to them for the kindness they extended to me. They are, indeed, the embodiment of the soul of Colorado that I recognize in this book and appreciate every day. Their actions and kindness have inspired me.

Thanks go out to my Gamma 2 Robotics work family for the last few years: Jennifer Folaron, Derek Euchler, Jason Collins, Justin Davis, Brian Alleman, and Brian Johnson. We went for quite a ride together.

My thanks to the team that helped make this book a reality: Mary Hoekstra, my editor, was relentless in reminding me that "it's all about the reader," and always asked the right questions to help me stay on point. Sebastian, my book designer, has worked with me since 2011 and has always found creative ways to present my work. And another "thank you" to John Brackney for his insightful read-through from a Colorado native's perspective.

Thanks to my daughter, Vanessa, who also came to the mountains. She has participated in one way or another in every book I have written, contributing cover art, cover ideas, and photos. Thank you for your love and creativity.

Hugs and thanks to my wife, Maura, who traveled with me to the mountains and was just as enamored as we shared in the joys of hiking, biking, and enjoying our new mountain life. Thank you for your love, support, and inspiration.

Jeff Pasquale is an Executive and Life Coach specializing in the areas of Life, Leadership, and Legacy.

He lives in Denver, Colorado

More information about Jeff can be found at www.JeffPasquale.com